GARY JONES

Athens Travel Guide

Contents

Introduction

Athens is one of the oldest cities in the world. It was once the home of the ancient Gods and Goddesses. It is the birthplace of Western civilization and democracy. It's a land of ancient temples, theaters, and even the Olympic Games. It is a historical and cultural melting pot.

This city is a combination of old and new. It has captivating ancient temples and a fair share of urban monoliths. You could climb up to the Acropolis to see the breathtaking panoramic view of the city. It was also once the home of the most brilliant minds in the world.

Athens is definitely a memorable travel destination that you should visit at least once in your lifetime.

This book is your ultimate travel guide to the ancient city of Athens. In this book, you'll find all the information you'll need to organize a 3 days Athens trip, including:

- Athens' rich and fascinating history
- What's the best time to go
- How to get around the city
- The most interesting and stunning cafes in the cities
- The most thought-provoking and visually stimulating museums
- The most famous landmarks in the city
- Where to eat
- The best budget friendly hotels
- Things that you can only do in Athens
- The best night bars and clubs
- Travel and safety tips
- Insider tips that will help you get the most out of your trip
- And more!

This book has everything you need to keep your trip fun, interesting, and hassle free. Athens is one gem of a city. It's filled with stunning historical sites that would definitely leave a mark in your memory. This book will give you all the information you need, so you would not miss everything that this wonderful and unforgettable city has to offer.

Thank you again for downloading this book and I hope that you enjoy it!

1

Athens: The Birthplace of Democracy and Western Civilization

Athens is one of the most marvelous cities that you'll ever visit in your lifetime. It is the birthplace of the democracy and Western civilization.

We wouldn't be able to enjoy the opportunity to choose our own leaders if it's not for the great minds of the Athenians. It is also the center of philosophy, cartography, geometry, and the Olympic. There's something about this lovely city that puts you in a meditative state. It is an intellectual center as much as it is a cultural hot spot. It was the home of some of the greatest minds of the history of mankind, including Socrates, Plato, and Solon. It was also once the home of the greatest philosopher of the ancient times – Aristotle.

Athens is one of the most scenic cities in the world. At its center lies the great Acropolis, the great ancient city which was once the political and religious center of Greece.

Today, Athens is the home of countless museums, universities, shopping malls, government buildings, and interesting neighborhoods. It's a place where the old meets the new. It's truly a wonderful and glorious place. No adjective is enough to describe its mystery, beauty, and glory.

The Rich History of Athens

Athens was thousands of years ahead of its time. It was the center of creativity, power, and ambition. It is a city of intellects, philosophers, and geniuses. It was often called the Ancient Silicon Valley.

The "city of the violet crown" got its name from its patron goddess – Athena. According to the legends and myths found in the works of Ovid, Herodotus, and Plutarch, both Poseidon (the god of the sea) and Athena (the goddess of wisdom) wanted to be the patron of the city. And so, a contest was held to determine which god is worthy of becoming the city's patron.

Poseidon made a spring in the middle of the city. This symbolizes naval power. Athena, on the other hand, created an olive tree which symbolizes wealth and peace. Cecrops, the mythical king of the city, accepted Athena's gift and named the city after her. It was said that the tree was located at the top of the Acropolis.

According to historians, a number of people lived in the city during the New Stone Age at the end of 4th millennium BC. By 1412 BC, Athens has become the center of the Mycenaean Civilization or the "bronze age". By this time, the Athenians built a Mycenaean fortress on the Acropolis. This is the foundation of Western Civilization. This fortress has Cyclopean walls and you could still a part of these walls today.

Ancient Greece

Athens was formerly ruled by Kings, including Cecrops I, Erichthonius, Pandion I, Theseus, and Apheidas. These kings were the leaders of the land-owning aristocracy called "Eupatridae", meaning well-born. For years, the rich families ruled in Athens. During this time, there was an ongoing conflict between the poor and the rich. To resolve this conflict, an aristocrat named Solon created a set of rules called the Solonian Law. He removed the privileges of the rich families and divided the Athenians into four classes. Each class has a separate governing body. Each class can elect officials. Solon created a set of rules called the Solonian Law. This law allowed more people to participate in the government. This is the start of what is now known as "democracy".

The 5th century BC is considered the "golden age" of the city. It was the time when the Parthenon was built. The Athenian art and philosophy were thriving during this time. But, the golden age ended when a war erupted between the Sparta and the Athenians.

By the 2nd century BC, Greece was under the power of the Roman Empire. The Romans ruled Greece for 500 years, but even during this time, Athens continued to be the home of philosophers, mathematicians, and intellectuals.

Athens was under the Byzantine rule in 529 AD. Constantine I founded the Byzantine Empiere and it's based in a city called Constantinople (now known as Istanbul). Byzantine art is mainly focused on religion. These artworks are colorful and have a mosaic-like texture. This was a great and prosperous period.

In 1204, the Latins conquered Athens and ruled until 1458, when it officially became a part of the Ottoman Empire.

The Greek revolution erupted in 1821 and Greece became an independent country in 1830. A Bavarian prince named Otto became the King of Greece. During this time, the residents of Athens lived in a quaint neighborhood named Plaka.

For a while Athens was a peaceful city until it fell in the hands of the Nazis during the World War II. It was a dark time for the city. But, after the war, Athens began to grow as many people around Europe and Asia migrated to the city, looking for better opportunities. Greece experienced a huge debt crisis in 2010. This led to unemployment and reduced pensions.

However, even if Athens went through an economic crisis, it remained as one of the most beautiful cities in the world.

2

Things You Need to Know Before Visiting Athens

Athens is a picture-perfect city with beautiful sights, marble temples, palace-like government buildings, fascinating museums, quirky restaurants, and even street art.

If you're traveling to Athens for the first time, below are a few things that you need to know.

The Athens Weather

Like most European cities, Athens has all the four seasons. It doesn't get too hot during the summer. It almost feels like you're in a tropical country. The Acropolis looks golden under the summer sun. It's also the best time to go to the beach and just enjoy the beauty of the flowers and the warmth of the turquoise sea.

If you're traveling to Athens during the summer months, make sure to bring an umbrella or a hat. It is the perfect time to take a day trip to fabulous Greek Islands such as Aegina, Hydra, and Spetses.

Athens is blooming in spring time. The weather is temperate – not too cold, not too hot. It's the perfect time to walk around the city and just enjoy the panoramic Athenian view. Tourist spots can get a little crowded during this time, though.

Athens looks stunning during the autumn season. The Acropolis is perched above a sea of beautiful building and red, purple, yellow, brown, and pink trees. The weather is cooler in October. Some autumn days are so warm that you'll think it's still summer time.

The winter in Athens is not at all brutal. The temperatures are usually range from 7 degrees Celsius to 18 degrees Celsius. The Acropolis almost looks like a ghost town during winter time. Hence, if you want to avoid the tourist groups and get good hotel rates, you should visit Athens in the winter.

Below are Athens' average temperatures by month:

Month Average Temperature in Celsius

December 11 degrees

November 14 degrees

October 18 degrees

September 24 degrees

August 28 degrees

July 29 degrees

June 20 degrees

May 19 degrees

April 16 degrees

March 12 degrees

February 10 degrees

January 9 degrees

Best Time To Visit Athens

Athens is most beautiful during the summer time. But, during this time, temperatures can go up to 33 degrees Celsius. Days can get too hot. This is also the city's tourism peak, so the hotel rates are expensive, and the tourist spots are filled with tourists. This is the reason why the best time to visit Athens is between March and May (Spring) and between September to November (Autumn).

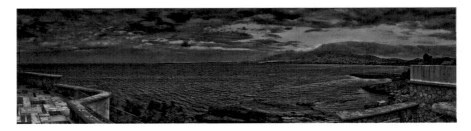

3

Transport And Safety

Athens has a well-developed transport system, making it easier to go around. There are a number of ways to get around the city – rental cars, the metro, buses, trolleys, trams, and taxis.

Athens International Airport Website
https://www.aia.gr/traveler/

Metro

The best way to explore Athens is through the subway/metro. The Athens metro has three lines, namely:

- 1 The Green Line (route: Piraeus to Kifisia; passes through 24 stations)
- 2 The Red Line (route: Anthoupoli to Elliniko; passes through 20 stations, this takes you to the touristy areas)
- 3 The Blue Line (route: Agia Marina to Doukissis Palakentias; passes through 20 stations)

These trains connect the most popular landmarks in Athens. You could find train stations in "touristy" neighborhoods.

Buses and Trolleys (Electric Buses)

Buses and trolleys are popular in Athens. More than 300 bus lines operate from 6am to 11pm in the city. But, buses traveling from the Athens Airport to the Port of Piraeus and Syntagma usually operate 24 hours. The regular buses are usually blue, and the trolleys are yellow.

Tram

Tram

Athens has a tram network system that has three lines and 48 stops. There are three tram lines and routes, namely:

- 1. Blue (route: Faliro Metro Station to Asklippio Voulas; passes through 31 stops)
- 2. Red (route: Faliro Metro Station to Syntagma; passes through 28 stops)
- 3. Green (route: Syntagma to Asklippio Voulas; passes through 37)

Taxi

You can easily find taxis everywhere in the city. A regular 3-kilometer ride usually costs 5.72 euros.

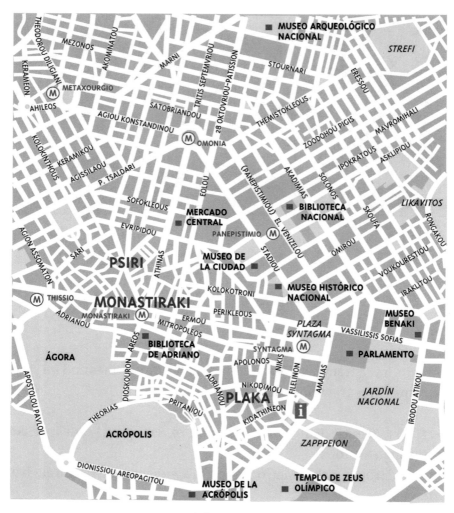

Athens Map

Safety and Travel Tips

Athens is generally safe. It's even great for lone female backpackers. But, like many metropolitan cities, some areas in Athens are filled with pickpockets and thieves.

Athens is a popular tourist spot, so it's no surprise that you could find a lot of pickpockets in the city. There are con artists preying on tourists in the city's major landmarks, especially the Acropolis. Beware of people offering to carry your luggage, some of these people may be thieves.

Keep an eye on your personal belongings, especially if you are on a bus or a train. Also, there are a lot of taxi scams around the city. There are cab drivers who set higher rates for foreigners. Some taxi drivers also pretend to forget to turn on the meter, so they can charge more than they should. There are also a lot of scammers in bars and club, so be careful. It is hard to spot scammers because some are well-dressed and well-mannered.

Here's a list of travel tips that can help make your Athens vacation more fun and hassle-free:

1.If you're on a tight budget, stay in hostels. This is also a good place to meet new friends.

2.Meals in touristy Plaka could cost around 40 euros. But, cafés usually charge around 12 euros. If you're on a budget, try street food. A lot of street vendors sell pizzas and gyros (Greek shawarma) for only 4 euros.

3.Dine at Plaka at least once. It's an expensive place but the food is worth the price.

4.Cash is king in Greece. When you're traveling to Athens, make sure that you have enough Euros. A few stores take cards.

5.Athens is a smoking city, so expect to see smokers everywhere.

6.Nightlife in Athens starts late. A lot of locals go out at 1 am or 2 am.

7.Most restaurants collect service fees, so you don't have to give tips.

8.Learn some commonly used Greek words:

- Good morning – Kalimera
- Good night – Kalinitha
- Good evening – Kalispera
- Thank you – Efharisto
- Hello – Ya or yassas
- Please – Parakalo
- Excuse me – Signomi
- Do you speak English – Milatay Agglika?
- I don't speak Greek – The milao ellinika.

9.Greeks usually close their stores at noon for their siesta break. So, if you need to buy something, do it in the morning.

10.Most tourist attractions are within walking distance from each other. You can save money when you walk from one place to another. Wear something comfortable when you around the Acropolis and Plaka. Most streets are elevated and located on the slopes of a mountain.

Finally, just enjoy the experience. Take as much photos as you can and live in the moment. You are, after all, in one of the most interesting and enchanting cities in the world.

4

The Best Tourist Spots in Athens

Athens has a rich (and almost mythical) history. It is the land of gods and goddesses. It was once the home of the wisest philosophers in the history. This modern city looks like a sea of skyscrapers and urban monoliths. But, some parts of the city gives you a glimpse of what Ancient Greece is like and why it was way ahead of its time.

Acropolis

The Acropolis and its Three Grand Structures – the Parthenon, the Propylaea, and the Erechtheion

The Acropolis is in every traveler's bucket list. This ancient city is nestled on a massive rock overlooking the quaint neighborhoods of Athens. The Acropolis is the foundation of Western Civilization. It's a complex of temples dedicated to their gods. It is the highest point of the city, about 150 meters above ground.

The Acropolis is the crowning glory of Athens and its most important landmark.

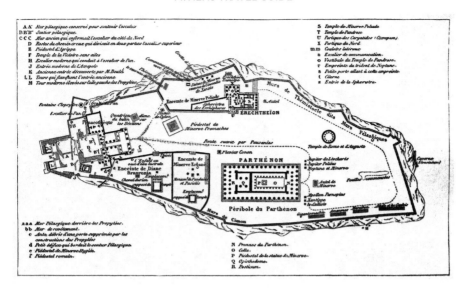

Old Map of Acropolis

There used to be a large fortress in Acropolis. But, today, all that's left are stone walls. But, you could still see the ruins of three grand structures – the Propylaea, the Erechtheion, and the great Parthenon.

The Propylaea is the grand entrance of the Acropolis. It was built to protect the ancient city from its enemies. It used to have five gates and it's supported by large Greek columns.

Propylaea

There's something about the Propylaea that's captivating. It makes you feel like you're entering a mystical world of beautiful Greek women, brave soldiers, and folklores.

The Erechtheion is an old temple located north of Acropolis. It's built for both Poseidon and Athena. This is one of the most elegant temples you'll ever see. It has a classic Ionic architecture. The columns are slender, and the carvings are intricate. This temple is still a beautiful and fascinating, so could just imagine how glorious it looked like during the ancient times.

Erechtheion

This temple has a room that houses the sacred olive wood statue of Athena. According to the myth, this statue was dropped from heaven. The most beautiful part of this building is the Porch of the Caryatids which features six statues of beautiful maidens functioning as columns. This is a proof of the ancient Greeks' creativity.

The most important temple on the Acropolis is the Parthenon. This striking temple was built in honor of the Goddess Athena – the patron of Athens. Parthenon literally means "an unmarried woman's apartment". It was believed that the goddess of strategy was a virgin.

Parthenon

This temple is made of marble. It has sophisticated architecture that's ahead of its time. It was completed in 432 BCE. The Parthenon has a classic Doric architecture (with a few Ionic elements). This means that the columns are thick and huge. This building is so stunning that it became the design inspiration for temples in Italy. It is also the design inspiration for many buildings in Washington, D.C., including the Jefferson Memorial, the National Gallery of Art, and the US Supreme Court.

The Temple of Olympian Zeus

Zeus was the supreme ruler of the sacred Mount Olympus. He was also known as the all-powerful god of war. He had two brothers – Poseidon (the god of the sea), and Hades (the god of the underworld). He was one of the greatest figures in Greek mythology, so it's no surprise that a number of temples were built in his honor.

The Temple of Olympian Zeus is about half a kilometer away from the Acropolis. It was built in 6th century BC, but it was completed in the 2nd century AD during the reign of the great Roman Emperor Hadrian.

The temple has gigantic Corinthian marble columns that will take your breath away. It's open for visitors from 8 am to 3 pm and the admission fee costs 6 euros. You can reach this temple via train (Akropolis, line 2).

The Ancient Agora of Athens

At the foot of the Acropolis, you'll find the Agora. This used to be the shopping mall of the ancient Athens.

Athenians regularly gathered here for three thousand years. It was the hub of ancient entrepreneurs and capitalists. It was the center of the city's economy. It was the foundation of Western economics, mathematics, and logic.

What's left of the Ancient Agora was turned into a museum. This museum showcases the sculptures and the artifacts found in the ancient marketplace. It is located at the restored Stoa of Attalos, the place where Socrates preaches about the virtue of temperance. It is also a place where Plato used to hang out. The Ancient Agora of Athens gives you a unique experience – it allows you to stand in the same ground where the greatest philosophers once stood.

Agora

This amazing marketplace used to be the center of Athenian politics, commerce, justice, and culture.

Aside from the museum, there are a lot of things that you can see in Ancient Agora, including:

- The Tower of the Winds – This marble clock tower was a horologion – a tool that ancient Greeks used to tell time. This tower was built by a Macedonian astronomer named Andronicus of Cyrrhus. This tower has interesting carvings and it has a number of features, including a wind vane, a water clock, and a sundials.

- The East Propylon – This is the eastern entrance of the Ancient Agora. It was built in 19 BC. Today, all that's left is a bunch of columns.

- Fethiye Mosque – This Ottoman mosque is a beautiful place of worship found at the northern part of the Ancient Agora. It's just a few steps from the Tower of the Winds. This Byzantine church was built in the 17th century and it has a stunning Ottoman architecture.

Fethiye Mosque

Syntagma Square

The Syntagma Square is open to the public. It is located at Pl. Sintagmatos, Athens. It was named after the first Greek constitution. It has a grand fountain and it's surrounded by five-star hotels and shops. It's also the home of the stunning Parliament House.

The Parliament Building was built in 1836 and it was completed in 1842. It used to be the Royal Palace of King Otto. This building has a neoclassical architecture and it is probably one of the most beautiful buildings you'll ever see in your lifetime. There's something about this building that's intimidating and, at the same time, captivating. It symbolizes power and the great wealth Greece used to have.

Syntagma Square

You could also find a lot of stores in Syntagma Square including H &M and Nike, so it's a great place to shop.

Syntagma Square – Greek Soldier

The Panathenaic Stadium and the Olympic Stadium

Panathenaic Stadium

It's no secret that the Olympic Games started as a religious activity held in Olympia to honor the Greek god Zeus. This tradition started in 776 BC. This sporting competition was held every four years for almost 12 centuries.

The Panathenaic Stadium is a multi-purpose stadium located at Leof. Vasileos Konstantinou. It is a cultural monument and for many years, this stadium hosted track events involving nude male athletes.

The Panathenaic Stadium opened in 556 BC. It is also called Kallimar-maro, which means "made of marble". It was the site of the first ever Olympic Games in 1896.

This stadium is an architectural masterpiece. It is a testament of the excellent Greek craftsmanship.

Panathenaic Stadium

If you're more into modern sports arena, head to the Olympic Stadium. This magnificent stadium was built in 1980 and it was opened in 1982. But, it was renovated in 2002 for the 2004 Olympic Games. It was no doubt one of the grandest Olympic Games in the history. The stadium has a football field and 9-lane race tracks. It has two electronic scoreboards. It is definitely one of the most beautiful stadiums in Europe.

The Olympic Stadium is also the site of many European and Greek sports competitions. Madonna held her concert at this huge Olympic Stadium in 2008.

5

Things That You Can Do Only in Athens

Most European cities look the same – they're filled with spectacular churches and magical palaces. But, Athens is different. You won't see fairytale like castles and elaborate fountains. You won't see the grand buildings that you're most likely to find in Krakow, Copenhagen, Serbia, and Paris. You won't see the medieval castles you can find in Wales, Bavaria, Prague, England, Dublin, and Edinburgh. But, there are also a few of awesome things that you can only do in Athens. Below is a list of the unique things that you can only do in Athens.

Explore the Vibrant Ancient Village of Plaka

Plaka is one of the most beautiful places you'll ever see. It is nestled in the northern and eastern slopes of the Acropolis It's quaint and colorful. It's definitely one of the most photogenic communities in the world. Every corner is picture perfect. This community is not open to cars, so you have to walk or bike around this neighborhood.

Plaka

Plaka is filled with vividly colored buildings and whimsical restaurants. The streets are lined with bright and vivid bougainvilleas. It's like you are transported to a different time or world. Plaka exudes nothing but good vibes! It is colorful and vivid. There's something about this neighborhood that's captivating – it can be the gleaming houses, the magnificent balconies decorated with flowers, or the quirky souvenir shops. But, whatever it is, there's something about Plaka that's truly magical.

This enchanting neighborhood is located on the slopes of a rocky mountain. This means that you have to climb stairs to explore the neighborhood. These stairs are lined with beautiful houses and cafes.

Plaka

Aside from the beautiful Cycladic houses, there are a lot of other things that you can see around this stunning neighborhood, such as:

1.Canellopoulos Museum

This museum showcases the vast art collection of the wealthy Canellopoulos Museum. It contains more than six thousand artifacts from prehistoric Greek civilization. It's also the home of a few modern artifacts. It's located at 12 Theorias Street, Plaka.

2.Anafiotika

This is a small neighborhood that's right under the Acropolis. This old town has breathtaking views. The houses in this neighborhood have a classic Cycladic architecture. This means that the houses have strong white walls and bright blue windows and doors. This neighborhood makes you feel like you're in a magical Greek island like Santorini or in Crete.

Anafiotika

Anafiotika

3.Frissiras Museum

This museum is located on Kidathinaion Street. It has a fascinating neoclassical architecture that's easy on the eyes. It also houses over three thousand sculptures, drawings, and paintings.

Shop in an Ancient Flea Market Called Monastiraki

Monastiraki is one of the top shopping spots in Athens. It is a square that's has flea market stores, bargain shops, an Ottoman mosque, and an old Greek Church.

Monastiraki

Monastiraki is a paradise for budget shoppers and treasure hunters. You can find beautiful and unique items at this flea market. You could find old books, sun glasses, furniture, second-hand clothes, fruits, accessories, figurines, jackets, furs, and even Greek flags.

Monastiraki

This area is not only great for shopping, it's also good for sightseeing.

There are a number of historical sites in the area, including:

1.Hadrian's Library – Roman Emperor Hadrian had this built. The library was the home of rolls of papyrus. It used to have a reading room. But, today, it's just a bunch of walls and columns.

Hadrian's Library Map

2.Church of Pantassa – This cathedral used to be attached to a monastery and it's facing the Monastiraki Station.

3.Tzistarakis Mosque – This beautiful mosque was built in 1759. It has a classic Ottoman architecture filled with arches and domes. It used to be a worship house, a storehouse, and a prison. But, it's now used as a museum showcasing the Greek Folk Art.

Tzistarakis Mosque

Meditate in the Athens National Garden

The Athens National Garden is located at Amalias 1, Athens. It's just a few steps away from the Syntagma Square. This garden is a lot simpler than other European gardens. It's peaceful and quiet – perfect for meditation. It has more than seven thousand trees and more than four thousand bushes. It's a paradise for nature lovers and botanists. This garden is the home of unique plants including the Canary Island date palms and the Chinese "trees of heaven".

Zappeion In National Gardens

This garden has six lakes with swans and ducks. If you're tired of walking around the busy city all day, this garden is your perfect escape.

Climb the Lycabettus Hill

The Lycabettus Hill (or Mount Lycabettus) is one of the popular tourist spots in Athens. It is the home of the Lykovatias Forest. It's 277 meters above the ground, making it one of the highest spots in the city. According to a legend, the goddess Athena carried the rock from Pentelis to the Acropolis. But, before she reached the ancient mountain, she heard that two of her servants opened the basket containing an infant named Erichthonius (which would later become a king). Athena was so mad that she dropped the rock. The rock later became the Lycabettus Hill.

Lycabettus Hill

This limestone rock has a theatre and a restaurant. It also has an amphitheater which was the venue of the concerts of well-known international artists like Vanessa Mae, the Pet Shop Boys, James Brown, Bjork, and Tracy Chapman.

This stunning hill is also the home of the Church of St. George. This church has a pure white exterior, but it has a colorful interior. The ceiling is decorated with beautiful paintings and an elegant chandelier.

It's something that you should take time to see.

But, what makes the hill special is not the church or the theatre – it's the breathtaking panoramic view of the Acropolis and the entire city.

You can get to this hill by driving a car, there's a parking space next to the theatre. You can also climb up the hill on foot or if you're not into hiking, you can take the cable car.

Cruise Around the Islands of Poros, Hydra, and Aegina from Athens

One of the great things about Athens is that it's just a few hours away from beautiful Greek Islands. It's no secret that Greece is the home of some of the most fabulous beaches in the world. If you're a certified beach lover, you should take a day trip to the Saronic Islands - Aegina, Hydra, and Poros.

Hydra

Hydra is just two hours away from Athens via the Port of Piraues. This small Saronic Island is dazzling and ravishing. All you could see is yellow, green, and blue. It has picturesque villages and relaxing beaches. It's one of the popular day trips from Athens.

It was once the home of the notorious Saronic pirates. One of the special things about this island is that cars are generally not allowed, so you have to explore it by foot.

Spetses is one of the breathtaking Saronic Islands. It is approximately an hour and forty-five minutes from Athens. It's known for its rock buildings, green mountains, and captivating blue waters.

Aegina is three hours from Athens and it has stunning views that will definitely take your breath away. It's also the home of the stunning Temple of Aphaea.

Aegina

You can visit one of these islands if you decide to do the daytrip on your own. But, a lot of travel agencies offer day cruises to these three islands from Athens. So, to make the best out of your trip, it's good to take a day cruise to these three islands. You could find a lot of day cruise boats at the Port of Piraues, but it's still best to book ahead online or by phone.

Statue of Apollo Athens

6

Top 5 Affordable Hotels in Hotels

Athens is a popular tourist spot, so it's filled with grand and luxurious hotels. Most of these hotels have rooftop pools overlooking the

Acropolis. These hotels have extravagant spas, gyms, restaurants, and bars. The rooms are so grandiose that they make you feel like a royalty. But, these hotels can cost an arm and a leg.

Fortunately, Athens is also filled with homey, amazing, and affordable hotels. Below is the list of the best budget friendly hotels in the "city of the violent crown".

The Stanley

The Stanley Athens has a captivating modern exterior. Rooms are complete with modern amenities. The rooms have a good view of the Acropolis. This hotel also has a few function rooms that are perfect for conferences, seminars, parties, and weddings.

This four-star hotel is situated in a busy and touristy area. It's just a few steps away from the Metaxourgeio Metro Station. It's located at Odysseos 1 – Karaiskaki Sq, Athens. And the best thing about this hotel is that it's affordable. You could stay in this luxurious hotel for only $69 a night.

Phone: +30 21 1990 0900

Hermes Hotel

Hermes Hotel is located at the heart of the busy Plaka neighborhood. It is located at Apollonos 19, just a few steps from the Acropolis. This modern three-star hotel is classy, comfortable, and easy on the eyes. It has a roof garden, a cozy lounge, and stunning restaurant that serves continental dishes. The hotel offers free Wi-Fi. It also has a bar and a playroom. They offer a breakfast buffet, too.

The rooms are cozy, warm, and comfortable and they all have

immaculate marble bathrooms. This hotel has excellent service and affordable prices. Rooms cost at least $83 a night. This hotel is perfect for those who want to spend a lot of time in Plaka.

Phone: +30 21 0322 2706

Polis Grand Hotel

Polis Grand Hotel has a modern and hip exterior. The rooms are so cozy that they almost make you feel like you're at home. Its balcony restaurant overlooks the Acropolis and gives you a good panoramic view of this stunning city. It's perfect for romantic dates. It serves buffet breakfast.

This four-star hotel is located at 19 Patision and 10 Veranzerou St., Athens. It's affordable, too. Hotel rooms cost at least $84.70.

Phone: +30 21 0524 3156

Socrates

The Socrates Hotel is located at Neofytou Metaxa 27 – 29, Athens. This three-star hotel has an easy access to the tourist neighborhood of Plaka. It's a few minutes from the Parthenon and the Acropolis. It's also a short walk away from the Omonoia Square and Monastiraki traditional market.

This quaint hotel has interesting walls that's look good on your Instagram feed. It also has a great bar and a "24/7" room service. It's affordable, too. You can book a twin or double room for as low as $40.60.

Phone: +30 21 0884 2211

Attalos Hotel

Attalos Hotel has an eclectic façade and a simple exterior. It is just one hundred meter from the Monastiraki Train Station. It has comfortable and elegant rooms. It has a breakfast buffet area and a rooftop bar where you could witness the glory of the Acropolis. It is just a five-minute walk to Ermou, the busiest shopping street in Athens.

Attalos Hotel is located at 29 Athinas Street, Athens. It's a touristy neighborhood lined with stores and quaint shops. This three-star hotel is just amazing and it's affordable, too. You can book a room for as low as $57.

To get the best rates, you should book ahead. It's also wise to visit Athens during off-peak season (autumn or early spring).

Phone: +30 21 0321 2801

7

The Greek Gastronomical Experience: The Top Five Restaurants in Athens

There's something about Greek food that keeps you begging for more. Greek dishes are delicious and healthy. It's filled with seafoods, fishes, and vegetables. You could try various dishes like Amygdalota, Baklava, Bougatsa, Courgette Balls, Galaktoboureko, and of course, the famous Greek Salad.

Athens has a string of fabulous restaurants that cater to every taste and budget. Below is the list of the top 5 restaurants that you should visit while in Greece.

Funky Gourmet

This restaurant has two Michelin stars. It is recognized as one of the best restaurants in the world. It is a hip, modern restaurant located in Paramithias, Gazi. This place is perfect for those who like Mediterranean food. The Funky Gourmet serves creative and out of this world dishes such as a fish fillet dipped in white chocolate and exotic lobster. The restaurant opened in 2007 and it has been on fire since. Meals usually cost $150, a bit pricey. But, it's all worth it.

The Funky Gourmet exudes elegance and opulence. It's innovative and it has a glass ceiling that gives you a good view of the sky. The food presentation is just amazing, and the desserts are too pretty to eat. Don't forget to make a reservation before heading to Athens.

Address: 13 Paramithias str
Phone: +30 21 0524 2727

Strofi

The best thing about Strofi is that it gives you a good view of the Acropolis. It's located in Rovertou Galli. This restaurant serves authentic Greek and Mediterranean cuisine. It has an impressive wine list, too. It was established in 1975 and it has been one of the most popular restaurants in Athens since then.

Strofi serves delicious food at an affordable price. Don't forget to try the fried feta cheese, steak in oregano sauce, and cheese baked eggplant.

Address:Rovertou Galli 25
Phone:+30 21 0921 4130

The Old Tavern of Psarras

The Old Tavern of Psarras is one of the few touristy restaurants where Greeks dine. So, if you want to eat like a local, head to this place. This romantic restaurant has an outdoor area that leads to the Acropolis.

Psarras serve authentic Greek traditional cuisine. Don't miss the chance to try the classic Greek salad and stuffed vine.

Address: Erechtheos 16
Phone:+30 210 3218734

Varoulko

This seaside restaurant has everything you could ever ask for – good food and breathtaking views. This restaurant is located in Akti Koumoundourou, Mikrolimano. It serves delicious seafood soups, garlic shrimps, and eggplant salad. Varoulko has that breezy Greek ambiance that exudes nothing but good vibes.

Address: Akti Koumoundourou 52
Phone:+30 21 0522 8400

Spondi

Spondi is a luxury two Michelin star restaurant located in Pyrronos 5, Pagkrati. It has a classic Mediterranean interior with whitewashed rock walls and interesting chandeliers. It's great for dates and anniversaries. The restaurant also has an outdoor dining area where guests can enjoy good food and the cold breeze of Athenian wind.

Spondi opened in 1996 and founded by well-known Greek chef Apostolos Trastelis. It's a bit pricey (a full meal would cost about $100), but it's worth every cent. This restaurant serves interesting dishes, such as Wild Mushroom Foie Grass, Chocolate Coeur de Guanaja, and Lobster served with peaches, potatoes, and tarragon. They also have top notch customer service.

Address: Pirronos 5
Phone:+30 21 0756 4021

8

The Best Athenian Museums

The Acropolis and the historic center of Athens look like open-air museums. They are relics of the past. But, if you want to know more about the ancient Greek civilization, you should visit a few of the city's many museums. Here are the best 5:

Acropolis Museum

The Acropolis is, no doubt, the eternal symbol of Athens. It is an ancient city that sits on top of a rocky mountain. It is one of the most historical, glorious, and magnificent landmarks in the world. It is 150 meters above the ground, so you can see this glorious ancient metropolis from almost anywhere in Athens.

Acropolis Museum

If you want to know more about this ancient city, head to the New Acropolis Museum. This modern building looks nothing like the museums in Rome, Berlin, Paris, or Prague. It has a modern architecture that showcases the mathematical precision of ancient Greece. But, it houses the most magnificent and historical artworks made in the ancient city of Acropolis.

The museum was opened in 2009. It was designed by a well-known Swiss architect named Bernard Tschumi. There's something mysterious and captivating about this amazing museum. It has glass walls, so you could enjoy the view of the Acropolis while you're in the museum.

This modern museum is built on the site of an ancient archaeological city called Makrygianni neighborhood. You could still see the remains of this marvelous ancient neighborhood from the huge opening on the museum's entrance hall. You can also see this fascinating archaeological site through the glass floors of the museum interior. The Makrygianni neighborhood is a testament of how beautiful ancient Athens was. This relic captures about three thousand years of Athenian life.

The museum has permanent exhibitions, namely:

· **The Gallery of the Slopes of the Acropolis** .This is gallery is the first art exhibition you'll find in the museum. It showcases sculptures, artifacts, bath vases, decorative motifs, figurines, and perfume bottles from two sanctuaries located on the slopes of the sacred mountain – the ancient temple of Dionysos Eleuthereus and the Sanctuary of the Asclepios, a temple dedicated to Nymphe.

· **The Archaic Acropolis Gallery** .This is a three-dimensional exhibit. This means that you can see the artworks from all sides. The Archaic Acropolis Gallery showcases the ancient Athenian artworks from the Archaic period (7 BC to 480 BC).The artworks in this gallery are just exquisite and hauntingly beautiful. It's like you're transported to a different time and place. These artworks are proof that even in 7th BC, Athens has already a thriving economy and a rich intellectual and creative life. This wonderful city is definitely ahead of its time.

· **The Parthenon Gallery** .During its peak, Parthenon was popular as one of the most beautiful and powerful temples in the world.The Parthenon Gallery showcases the ancient artworks and scriptural decorations of this popular landmark.

- **The Artifacts of Propylaia, Athena Nike, and Erechtheion** .This gallery showcases the artworks of the main entrance of the Parthenon called Propylaia. This grand entrance housed magnificent sculptures by well-known artists such as Alkamekes. This gallery also houses the statues from other famous temples, such as the Erechtheion and Athena Nike.

- **From 5th CB to 5th AD** .There's something about this gallery that's haunting and captivating. You could walk amidst the ancient sculptures placed on marble pedestals. This gallery showcases the artworks from the Sanctuary of Artemis Brauronia. This part of the museum also houses popular artworks such as the portrait of Alexander the Great by Leochares. You could also find the statue of Prokne, the daughter of King Pandion of Attica and the statues of countless emperors, generals, orators, priests, and philosophers.

The Acropolis Museum is located at Dionysiou Areopagitou 15. It is open from 8 am to 8 pm during summer season (except on Mondays – the museum closes at 4 pm). During winter season, the museum is open from 9 am to 5 pm on most days. The entrance fee costs 5 euros.

Address:Dionysiou Areopagitou 15
Phone: +30 21 0900 0900

Benaki Museum

This museum was established in 1930 and it's housed inside the beautiful Benaki Museum located at Koumpari I, Athens. It's right across the National Garden. It was established in 1930 by famous Greek art collector Antonis Benakis in honor of his entrepreneur and politician father Emmanouil Benakis.

This museum has a classic architecture. But, when you go inside, you feel like you're transported to a time of extravagant dresses and lavish furniture.

Benaki Museum

The Benaki Museum has a wide collection of elaborate costumes. It also showcases the paintings of famous artists, such as Theodoros, Ioannis Permeniatis, El Greco, Michael Damaskenos, Emmanuel Tzanes, Nikolaos Kantounis, and Dionysios Solomos. It also features artworks and artifacts from Anatolia, Egypt, Arabian Peninsula, the Middle East, Persia, Mesopotamia, India, Sicily, Spain, and North Africa.

This museum has pure white walls and a number of amazing chandeliers. It houses more than 40,000 artworks and artifacts. It also has a museum souvenir shop and a snack bar that gives you a good view of the Parthenon.

The Benaki Museum is open from 10 am to 6 pm every Wednesdays and Fridays from 10 am to midnight every Thursdays and Saturdays. It is open from 10 am to 4 pm on Sundays and closed every Monday and Tuesday. The entrance fee costs 9 euros.

Address:Koumpari 1
Phone:+30 21 0367 1000

National Archaeological Museum

The National Archaeological Museum is the home of the most important archaeological artifacts in Greece from the prehistoric period to until the late antiquity (8 A.D.). It was established by Greek governor Ioannis Kaposdistrias.

This museum has a neoclassical Greek architecture. The building's façade is filled with intimidating columns. It has an impressive collection of gold artifacts, including the Mask of Agamemnon, Mycenean gold cups, and elliptical funeral head dresses. This museum is like a large treasure chest.

National Archaeological Museum

The National Archaeological is a paradise for Greek mythology fans. You could find stunning and ethereal statues of Greek gods and goddesses Zeus, Athena, Themis, Aphrodite, Asklepius, Dionysos, Pan, Eros, and Satyr. These statues are so beautiful that they look like they're floating on the exquisite marble floor.

You could also find a number of painted jars that depicted ancient war scenes and a huge bronze statue of a jockey riding a horse. Everything in this museum is absolutely magnificent and captivating.

This museum is located at 28is Oktovriou 44. It is open from 12 noon to 8 pm on Sundays and Mondays. It is open from Tuesday to Saturday from 8 am to 8 pm. The entrance fee costs 10 euros.

Address:28is Oktovriou 44

Phone:+30 21 3214 4800

Goulandris Museum of Cycladic Art

This museum has a mansion-like interior. It's housed in the Stathatos Mansion - one of Athens architectural gems. Its exterior exudes elegance and opulence. This museum is a great place to discover the spellbinding Greek history. We all know the Cycladic architecture – it's used all over Santorini. But, if you want to know more about Cycladic art, head to the Goulandris Museum.

The Goulandris Museum is known for its vast collect of Cycladic art – figurines that were created in the Aegan Islands during 3000 BC or the early "bronze age", the height of the Cyclandic culture.

You could find a lot of interesting minimalistic Cycladic marble sculptures produced during the Neolithic Period. Some of these sculptures look like violins, but in fact they are symbols of naked squatting women. These artworks symbolize the Ancient Greek's talent, culture, and creativity. These pieces of arts are carefully arranged in glass-protected installations. This museum magically fuses the old with the new.

This museum has different sections, namely:

1.Cycladic Art Collection

This section houses the most important Cycladic art collection in the world. It showcases nude marble statues that inspired artists like Henry Moore, Barbara Hepworth, Giacometti, Modigliani, and Brancusi.

2.Ancient Greek Art: History in Images

This section showcases the history of the Aegean societies. It features artworks and artifacts that symbolize the political, cultural, technological, and social development of Greek civilization. You would see jars, busts, warrior helmets, and other interesting artifacts.

3.Cyprus: Aspects of Ancient Art and Culture

This section showcases the ancient artifacts and sculptures from Cyprus. The artworks are rather interesting and thought provoking. This part of the museum also contains unique and intriguing treasures and jars from Cyprus – the island of Aphrodite. These artifacts are usually made of glass, gold, clay, silver, and bronze. Most of these artworks are part of the art collection of a wealthy Cyprian named Thanos Zintilis.

4.Scenes From The Daily Life in Antiquity

This is probably the most beautiful and interesting part of the Goulandris Museum. It showcases over 150 artifacts from Ancient Greece, including weapons, vases, and figurines. These artworks are divided into three five parts or themes – the Underworld, the World of Men, Eros, Gods, and Heroes.

The Goulandris Museum also has a temporary exhibition area where known artists like Sarah Lucas, Thomas Struth, Louise Bourgeois, Ai Weiwei, and Martin Kippenberger display their works.

This dazzling museum is located in Neofitou Douka 4, Athens. The entrance fee costs 7 euros (as of writing). It's open from 11 am to 9 pm on Sunday. It is also open from 10 am to 5 pm every Monday, Wednesday, and Saturday. It's open from 11 am to 8 pm on Thursdays and it is closed every Tuesday.

Address: Neofitou Douka 4

Phone:+30 21 0722 8321

Numismatic Museum of Athens

The Numismatic Museum is not as popular as the other museums in this list. But, it's a place you should not miss if you're in Athens. This museum has a fascinating Beaux-Arts architecture. It almost looks like a modern palace.

The museum interior has interesting designs and colors. The Byzantine and Christian paintings on the building's museum are captivating. This museum has one of the biggest collections of ancient coins. You could find rare and valuable coins and gems, including the gold coins of Epidaurus, Ancient Corinth, Sicily, and Byzantine Empire. These coins bear the image of kings, rulers, gods, and goddesses.

The exhibition rooms are exquisite and fascinating. These rooms look like they're part of a lavish European palace. This museum is a haven for coin collectors. But, it's also a paradise for book lovers. The museum has over twelve thousand books about archaeology, numismatics, and history.

The museum area also has a stunning garden with fascinating statues. It's a good place to just walk around and think about the good things in life.

The Numismatic Museum was founded in 1838, making it one of the oldest museums in Greece. It is located at Ilou Melatron, Eleftheriou Venizelou 12, Athens. It's open from 9 am to 4 am from Tuesday to Sunday. It's open from 1 pm to 8 pm every Monday. The entrance fee costs 6 euros.

Address:Eleftheriou Venizelou 12

Phone:+30 21 0363 2057

9

Exploring the Greek Art Scene: The Best Art Galleries

The contemporary Greek art is rather captivating and mind-puzzling. If you're into eclectic (and classic) art, you should check out the art galleries around Athens.

Ileana Tounta Contemporary Art Centre

This art gallery was founded in 1988 and it's the home of various contemporary artworks in Athens. This gallery has a simple industrial space that's decorated with interesting and thought provoking art.

The Ilean Tounta Contemporary Art Centre sometimes features the work of eclectic artists like Dimitrios Antonitsis, Eva Mitala, Katerina Kotsala, Frini Mouzakitou, and Ionna Pantazopoulou.

Address: Klefton 48

Deste Foundation for Contemporary Art

Deste Foundation is a gallery established by Dakis Joannou. This art gallery has an interesting exterior. This art gallery showcases odd and sometimes, mind-boggling art installations. You could also find a few paintings and photographs. This gallery is for those looking unique and eclectic art.

Address: Filellinon 11, Nea Ionia

Rebecca Camhi Gallery

This beautiful gallery is definitely one of the most beautiful and popular galleries in Athens. It was established in 1995 and it's housed in a stunning neoclassical building located in Leonidou 9. This gallery showcases the works of international artists like Nobuyoshi Araki, Rita Akermann, and Nan Goldin. It also showcases the work of famous Greek artists.

Address: Leonidou 9

CAN - Christina Androulidaki Gallery

This classy art space is located at Panagiotuo Anagnostopoulou 42, Athen. CAN was founded by Christina Androulidaki who has art and history degrees from the University of Edinburgh and the Courtauld Institute in London. This gallery is filled with white spaces that showcase the work of Maria Kriara, Lefteris Tapas, Alexis Vasilikos, Dimitris Condos, and Marianna Ignataki.

Address: Panagiotou Anagnostopoulou 42

Radio Athenes

This amazing museum was founded in 2014 by Andreas Melas and Helena Papadopoulos. It's a non-profit contemporary art gallery. It's located at the heart of the city, at 15 Petraki, Athens. It is also a bookstore and an event hall. The installations can be viewed from the outside with its clear glass wall. A lot of artists hang out here to find inspiration for painting and writing.

Address:Street, Petraki 15

View of Athens

10

Experience the Greek Coffee Culture: Best Coffee Shops in Athens

The Greek coffee (locally known as ellinikos kafes) is a powdered ground coffee served in half cups. It's a lot stronger than the regular coffee and it's brewed in a pot called briki. The baristas usually use a utensil called kaimaki to create foam. Coffee is a vital part of the Greek culture. It was used to predict the weather during the ancient times. Greeks believe that if the bubbles are clustered in the middle of the cup, it's going to be a sunny day. If the bubbles form around the mouth of the cup, it's going to rain. Also, frappe was invented in Greece during the 60s.

Today, the Athens is filled with fascinating and modern coffee shops. Some of these cafes even have world class bartenders. Below is a list of the best coffee shops in the city.

Tailor Made

Tailor Made is one of the first specialty coffee shops in Athens. It's located in Plateia Agias Eirinis that serves fresh roasted coffee from different parts of the world, including Ethiopia, Kenya, Brazil, Panama, Honduras, and Costa Rica. It also serves delicious home-made desserts, infusions, snacks, and teas. It's a good place to hang out. This café has an in-house DJ, too.

Tailor Made has a funky and electrifying urban interior that's cool and relaxing. The ambience is superb and the coffee is even more amazing.

Address: Agias Irinis 2
Phone: +30 21 3004 9645

Chaplin

Chaplin is one of those side street coffee shops around Athens.

Chaplin is one of the city's highest rated coffee shops and for a good reason. It has an interesting interior that's usually filled with Earth colors. It also has a photogenic giant chandelier that's perfect for your

Instagram feed. It also has an outdoor seating area perfect for people watching. This shop serves great coffee and superfood cocktails.

Address: Kalamiotou 16
Phone:+30 698 745 4777

The Underdog

The Underdog is located at Iraklidon 8. The coffee so good and it is the workplace award-winning barista named Michalis Dimitrakopoulus. This café has an interesting interior, a clean coffee bar, and delightful wooden stools. They serve cold beers, too. It's a perfect place to hang out.

Address: Iraklidon 8
Phone:+30 21 3036 5393

Taf Coffee

If you love coffee art, head to Taf Coffee located at Emmanouil Mpenaki 7. It was founded by Yiannis Taloumis in the 90s. This shop serves an award-winning espresso blend called Rosebud. Like the Underdog, Tag Coffee has an award-winning team, too. Their iced brew coffee is to die for. This coffee shop has become so successful that it has opened branches in Milan, London, and Singapore.

Address: Emmanouil Benaki 7
Phone:+30 21 0380 0014

Mind The Cup

Mind The Cup is a quaint little café located in Peristeri. If you want some quiet time, head to this place. It's pleasantly located away from the busy touristy streets. It has a funky street interior that will surely captivate your interest.

Mind The Cup is one of the best places to relax and just hang out. It has a great interior and it offers outdoor seating, too. The baristas are super friendly and then sometimes have a DJ, too.

Address:Emiliou Veaki 29
Phone:+30 21 0577 6010

11

The Best Bars in the City

Plaka

Greeks have a sophisticated taste. So, it's not surprising that the city is filled with classy, elegant, and interesting bars.

The night life in Athens is just as fascinating as its temples and historic sites. Below is a list of the best bars in the city.

Brettos

Established in 1909, Brettos is the oldest surviving bar in Athens and definitely one of the most beautiful bars you'll ever visit in your lifetime. Its walls are decorated with colorful bottles of wine and beer. The bar also features barrels of perfectly age wine.

The place serves two hundred fifty different cocktails and a hundred seventy Greek wines. It's definitely a paradise for picky beer drinkers and wine connoisseurs. This bar is located in Kidathineon 41, Athens. It's in the quaint and colorful Plaka neighborhood.

Phone:+30 21 0323 2110

Galaxy Bar

If you like good wine and you have a lot of money to burn, head to the Galaxy Bar. This bar is nestled on the top floor of Hilton Hotel in Athens. It allows you to drink a kick-ass cocktail while staring at the grandeur of the Acropolis.

The Galaxy Bar has an impressive wine list and stunning views. It's a great place to socialize or just enjoy a glass of exquisite wine.

This elegant bar is located at 46 Vassilissis Sofias Avenue, Athens. It is open from 7:30 pm until early morning.

Phone:+30 21 0728 1402

Seven Jokers

This elegant bar is a favorite after-work hangout area of many local young professionals. It's a place where hard-working millennials drink cold beer and eat finger foods after a long day at work. This bar is so beautiful that it feels like you're transported to the 1920s. Its walls are decorated with expensive wines. You could see elegant and colorful lamps hanging from the ceiling. This bar also has friendly and energetic bartenders and an impressive wine list.

You should visit this Instagram-worthy bar while in Athens. It's located at Voulis 7 and it's open from 6 pm until early in the morning.

Phone:+30 21 0321 9225

A For Athens Bar

A For Athens is a hip urban hotel next to the Monastriki train station. Its bar is becoming one of the best and most popular night hangouts in the city. This rooftop bar has the best view of the Acropolis.

The A for Athens Bar has friendly bartenders who serve fascinating cocktails with interesting names. Its head bartender, Theodore Pyrillos, was hailed the champion of the European Cocktail Competition.

This bar has a vibrant and vivid atmosphere that draws a long queue of guests each night. So, it's best to make a reservation.

Phone:+30 21 0324 4244
Address:Miaouli 2

The Clumsies

The Clumsies is known as one of the best bars in the world. It is housed inside a beautiful neoclassical building. It has an elegant interior and a team of world class bartenders. This bar serves "out of this world" cocktails that will give you a unique experience. These cocktails are not only delicious, they're also innovative and picture perfect.

This bar is open as early as 10 am and closes at 2 am. It is located in Praxitelous, Athens.

Phone:+30 21 0323 2682
Address:Praxitelous 30

12

Party Like A Greek: The Best Night Clubs in Athens

Greeks are nice, polite, and friendly people. They are energetic, and they love to have a good time. So, it's no surprise that Athens has an electrifying energetic nightlife. Below is the list of the night clubs that you should not miss in Athens.

Island

Island is one the most popular night clubs in Athens. It is the hub of jet-setting celebrities, socialites, and stylish locals. This club has a restaurant that serves the best international cuisines and inventive cocktails. It's definitely a place where you could dance and relax. It's a good place to meet new people, too.

This is located on Sounio Avenue, Variza, Athens Riviera, about 27 kilometers from downtown Athens.

Lohan Nightclub

Lohan Nightclub is one of the hottest nightclubs in Athens and yes, it's owned by Lindsay Lohan. It is located at 30, Iera Odos 32 and it's definitely one of the wildest clubs in the city. This club is a hedonist's paradise, a feast for the senses. You could see "black light" dancers, sexy vixens, and attractive party animals everywhere. The club features famous Greek DJs, too. It's a good place to cut loose and have a good time.

Phone: +30 698 750 1825

Dybbuk

Dybbuk exudes nothing but good vibes. It has a great combination of hypnotizing music and spectacular lights. It has been the center of Athens nightlife since 2009. It's located at the posh Loulkiano Street. It is the home of famous DJs like Agent Greg. This club also hosts dance shows every now and then.

There's something about Dybbuk that's electrifying and captivating. It is a great place to meet new people, too.

Bolivar Beach Bar

Bolivar Beach Bar is located on Poseidonos Avenue, Alimos. It's just 30 minutes away from the tourism center of Athens. This bar combines the best things in life – the beach, good music, good food, sun, cold beer, and beautiful people. It's the ultimate party destinations for tourists and Greek millenials. This place has amazing tiki huts and mind-blowing cocktails.

Phone: +30 697 036 7684

Steam

Steam is vibrant, energetic, and vivacious, just like the Athenian nightlife. This club is the site of many events and parties. It has an impressive list of amazing DJs, including Amalia Kalameniou and the Cosmic Boys. This club plays hypnotic music that makes you forget all your worries for a few hours.

Steam is located at Evrimedontos 3, Gazi and just a few steps away from the Karameikos Train Station.

Phone: +30 21 0341 2120

13

The Ultimate 3 Day Athens Travel Itinerary

Athens is the center of the Ancient Greece. It is filled with remnants of its rich cultural past. The city is the home to picturesque neighborhoods, jaw-dropping views, fascinating old temples, and stunning mosques. There are a lot of sites to visit, so below is a three-day travel itinerary that you can use to plan your trip:

Day 1- The Acropolis, Plaka, and Nearby Tourist Sites

- 1.Visit the Acropolis and its temples – the Propylaia, the Parthenon, the Temple of Athena Nike, and the Erechtheion.
- 2.Explore the ancient neighborhood of Plaka.
- 3.See the Ancient Agora.
- 4.Visit the Syntagma Square.
- 5.Meditate at the National Garden.
- 6.Shop at the Monastiraki market.
- 7.See the Acropolis Museum

Day 2 – Museums and the Lycabettus Hill

Lycabettus Hill

- 1.Visit the National Archaelogical Museum.
- 2.See the Benaki Museum.
- 3.Explore the Goulandris Museum of Cycladic Art.

- 4.Climb the Lycabettus Hill.

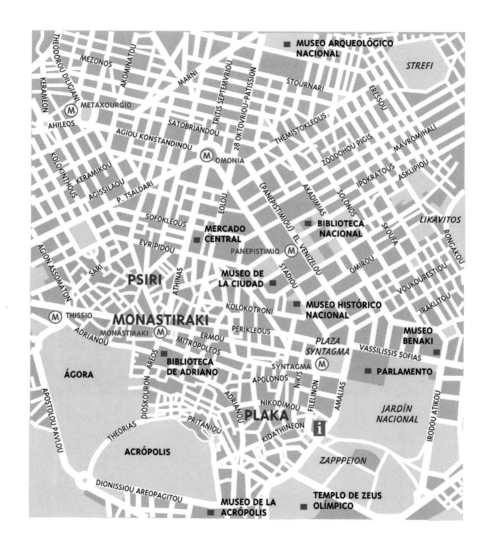

Day 3 – Day Trip to the Saronic Island

Take a day trip to the Saronic Islands of Hydra, Aegina, and Poros, especially if you're not planning to visit another Greek city or Island (Santorini, Crete, etc). These islands are just as stunning as the more popular Greek islands.

Aegina

If you have more time, take day trips to Cape Sounion, Olympia, and Meteora so you could see more fascinating temples and other tourist spots. Join discounted group tours. If you're a foodie, you can also join the classic Athens food tour. And most of all, if you're already in Athens, why not extend your stay in Greece and visit the stunning Mykonos or Santorini?

Hydra Island

14

Conclusion

Thank you for reading this book!

I hope that this book was able to help you plan a hassle-free and fun trip to Athens. Before traveling to Athens, here's a list of things that you should keep in mind:

- Before you travel, make sure that you have complete travel documents. Also, make sure that you have the contact number of your country's embassy in Greece.
- Book your hotel and ferry tickets ahead to get great deals.
- Use Booking.com to get great hotel discounts.
- Greece is a smoking country. So, you'll probably see people smoking anywhere.
- You can see stray animals anywhere. This can be a bit annoying for tourists.
- Don't forget to bring your camera – Athens is one of the most photogenic cities in the world.
- Invest in a good map. This will make your life easier.
- Take time to learn a few Greek phrases.
- Make sure that you have enough euros in your pocket. A lot of stores in Athens do not accept credit cards.
- Make sure that you are appropriately dressed before you enter a church.
- Pack light if you are traveling to another Greek island through ferry. Use a backpack. It's easier to carry around.
- Be kind. Greeks are kind people, but only if you're nice to them, too.
- Don't hesitate to ask for help.
- Be wary of scams.
- Most ATMs in Greece have a daily withdrawal limit.
- Don't forget to try Gyros (Greek shawarma-like snack) and the Kalamari (fried octopus).
- The tap water in Athens is generally safe. But, if you go out of Athens, drink bottled water.
- Always wear your seatbelt when you're in the car. Greeks are crazy drivers.
- You will need to pay toll fees if you're visiting multiple towns.
- Pharmacies are closed during weekends. So, make sure you have all

the medicine you'll need before the weekend.

- Drink a lot of water when you're in Athens, especially during summer time.
- A lot of Greek taverns do not have a closing time. They close when the last customer leaves!
- Check the inclusion of your hotel accommodation. A lot of hotels in Athens do not offer free breakfast.
- Greeks get annoyed when tourists publicly display their drunkenness, so it's important to drink moderately.
- Most road signs are written in Greek, so it's not advisable for tourists to rent a car and drive. Use public transportation instead.
- Take a day trip from Athens if you have more time.

And lastly, have fun! Enjoy every moment of your trip. Thank you again for downloading this book and good luck!

National Garden Of Athens

15

Thank You

I want to thank you for reading this book! I sincerely hope that you received value from it!

If you received value from this book, I want to ask you for a favour .Would you be kind enough to leave a review for this book on Amazon?

Made in the USA
Thornton, CO
04/08/24 18:58:10